EMMANUEL JOSEPH

Reclaiming Your Inner Strength: A Guide to Emotional Healing After Divorce

Copyright © 2023 by Emmanuel Joseph

All rights reserved. No part of this publication may be reproduced, stored or transmitted in any form or by any means, electronic, mechanical, photocopying, recording, scanning, or otherwise without written permission from the publisher. It is illegal to copy this book, post it to a website, or distribute it by any other means without permission.

First edition

This book was professionally typeset on Reedsy.
Find out more at reedsy.com

Contents

1	Chapter 1: The Emotional Rollercoaster of Divorce	1
2	Chapter 2: Building a Support System	4
3	Chapter 3: Self-Care During Divorce	7
4	Chapter 4: Grieving and Letting Go	10
5	Chapter 5: Rediscovering Your Identity	13
6	Chapter 6: Coping with Change and Uncertainty	16
7	Chapter 7: Healing through Forgiveness	19
8	Chapter 8: Co-Parenting and Communication	22
9	Chapter 9: Rebuilding Trust and Relationships	25
10	Chapter 10: Financial Recovery and Independence	28
11	Chapter 11: Setting New Goals and Aspirations	31
12	Chapter 12: Embracing a Brighter Tomorrow	34

1

Chapter 1: The Emotional Rollercoaster of Divorce

Divorce is a journey through uncharted emotional territory. It's a rollercoaster ride of feelings that can leave you exhilarated, terrified, and utterly drained, often all within the same day. In this chapter, we will delve into the complexities of the emotional landscape you are about to traverse and how to navigate it with resilience and self-compassion.

Understanding the Emotional Challenges

The decision to divorce is rarely taken lightly. It marks the end of a significant chapter in your life, and with that ending comes a flood of emotions. It's essential to recognize that experiencing a wide range of emotions is entirely normal. You might feel sadness, anger, fear, relief, guilt, confusion, and even moments of unexpected happiness. These emotions can be overwhelming, and they may take you by surprise.

Divorce often feels like a grieving process. You're mourning the loss of a partnership, a shared future, and sometimes, the dissolution of a family unit. Allow yourself to grieve. It's okay to cry, to be angry, and to feel lost. Emotions are a natural part of the healing process.

Acknowledging Your Feelings and Emotions

One of the first steps in coping with the emotional rollercoaster of divorce is acknowledging your feelings without judgment. It's easy to label certain emotions as "good" or "bad," but all emotions serve a purpose. Anger can motivate you to protect yourself, sadness can help you process loss, and even moments of happiness can offer relief amidst the turmoil.

Start by keeping a journal. Write down what you're feeling each day, even if it seems insignificant. This practice can help you identify patterns and triggers in your emotions. Over time, it can also serve as a powerful record of your progress.

Remember that healing is not a linear process. There will be days when you feel like you're making great strides, and others when you seem to slide backward. This is all part of the journey. Be patient with yourself.

Seeking Support

You don't have to navigate this emotional rollercoaster alone. One of the most crucial aspects of healing after divorce is building a strong support system. Friends and family can provide a shoulder to lean on, lend an empathetic ear, and offer practical help when needed.

Consider seeking professional support as well. A therapist experienced in divorce and its emotional aftermath can be a valuable resource. They can provide coping strategies, help you process your feelings, and offer guidance in setting goals for your healing journey.

In the chapters that follow, we'll explore various aspects of emotional healing after divorce in greater detail. Remember, you're not alone in this journey.

CHAPTER 1: THE EMOTIONAL ROLLERCOASTER OF DIVORCE

Your emotions are valid, and by acknowledging and addressing them, you're taking the first steps toward reclaiming your inner strength and building a brighter future.

2

Chapter 2: Building a Support System

Divorce can feel like a lonely and isolating experience, but it doesn't have to be. One of the most important steps in your journey toward emotional healing is building a strong and reliable support system. In this chapter, we'll explore the significance of seeking support from friends, family, and professionals, and how they can help you navigate the challenges of divorce.

The Importance of Seeking Support

Going through a divorce can be emotionally overwhelming. It's perfectly normal to feel a range of intense emotions, from sadness and anger to confusion and fear. These emotions can be difficult to handle on your own, which is why seeking support is essential.

1. Friends and Family: Your loved ones can provide a crucial source of emotional support. They know you well and can offer a listening ear, a comforting hug, or a distraction when you need it most. Don't hesitate to lean on them during this time. Share your feelings and concerns openly with those you trust.

2. Therapists or Counselors: Professional support is invaluable. A therapist or

counselor experienced in divorce can help you navigate the complex emotions and challenges you're facing. They can provide a safe and non-judgmental space for you to express yourself and offer guidance on coping strategies.

3. Support Groups: Joining a divorce support group can be incredibly beneficial. Meeting others who are going through similar experiences can provide a sense of belonging and understanding. It can also offer different perspectives and coping strategies.

Finding the Right Support

Not all support systems are created equal, and what works for one person may not work for another. Here are some tips for finding the right support:

- Choose Supportive and Non-Judgmental People: Surround yourself with individuals who are empathetic, understanding, and non-judgmental. Avoid those who may be critical or unsupportive of your choices.

- Consider Professional Help: If you're struggling to cope with intense emotions or find it challenging to talk to friends and family, a trained therapist or counselor can be your anchor.

- Explore Support Groups: Support groups can provide a sense of community and understanding. Look for groups that align with your needs, whether it's a general divorce support group or one focused on specific issues like co-parenting or healing from infidelity.

Balancing Independence and Support

While it's essential to seek support during this challenging time, it's also crucial to maintain your independence and self-reliance. Striking a balance between relying on others and taking ownership of your healing journey is key. Your support system is there to assist, not replace your inner strength.

In the chapters ahead, we will explore various aspects of emotional healing after divorce in more detail, including self-care, processing grief, and rebuilding your sense of self. Remember, building a support system is a vital step, and it's a sign of strength, not weakness, to reach out to others during this time.

3

Chapter 3: Self-Care During Divorce

Divorce is undeniably one of life's most challenging experiences, and it can take a significant toll on your emotional and mental well-being. During this turbulent time, prioritizing self-care is not a luxury; it's a necessity. In this chapter, we will explore the importance of self-care and provide practical strategies to help you nurture your emotional health as you navigate the divorce process.

Prioritizing Self-Care

Self-care is a deliberate and ongoing practice of tending to your physical, emotional, and mental needs. It's not about indulgence; it's about sustaining your well-being. Here's why self-care is crucial during divorce:

1. Emotional Resilience: Divorce can be emotionally draining. Self-care activities can help you recharge, manage stress, and maintain emotional resilience.

2. Coping Mechanism: Self-care provides healthy coping mechanisms to deal with the range of emotions that come with divorce, from sadness and anger to anxiety and uncertainty.

3. Self-Compassion: It's easy to be self-critical during this time. Self-care encourages self-compassion, reminding you to treat yourself kindly and without judgment.

Practical Self-Care Strategies

1. Establish a Routine: Create a daily routine that includes essential self-care activities such as exercise, nutritious meals, and sufficient sleep. Having structure can provide stability during a tumultuous time.

2. Exercise Regularly: Physical activity is a powerful stress reliever. Whether it's a daily walk, yoga, or hitting the gym, find an activity that you enjoy and make it a regular part of your routine.

3. Mindfulness and Meditation: Practicing mindfulness and meditation can help you stay grounded in the present moment and reduce anxiety. Even just a few minutes a day can make a difference.

4. Seek Professional Help: Don't hesitate to reach out to a therapist or counselor who specializes in divorce-related issues. Professional support can be a vital component of self-care.

5. Maintain Healthy Boundaries: Set boundaries with your ex-partner to protect your emotional well-being. This includes limiting contact when necessary and clearly defining your new post-divorce boundaries.

6. Engage in Activities You Love: Reconnect with hobbies and activities that bring you joy and fulfillment. Engaging in things you love can be a source of emotional nourishment.

7. Practice Self-Compassion: Be gentle with yourself. Acknowledge your feelings without judgment. Remember that it's okay to have bad days, and setbacks are a natural part of the healing process.

CHAPTER 3: SELF-CARE DURING DIVORCE

Self-Care as a Foundation

Think of self-care as the foundation upon which your emotional healing is built. When you prioritize self-care, you are better equipped to face the challenges of divorce with resilience and clarity. It's not selfish; it's self-preservation.

In the chapters ahead, we will explore various aspects of emotional healing after divorce, including processing grief, rebuilding your sense of self, and forging a path toward a brighter future. Self-care is your anchor throughout this journey, providing the strength and stability you need to emerge from divorce stronger and wiser.

4

Chapter 4: Grieving and Letting Go

Divorce marks the end of a significant chapter in your life, and with endings come a natural process of grieving. Grief is a complex emotional journey that encompasses a range of feelings, and acknowledging and navigating this process is crucial for emotional healing. In this chapter, we will explore the stages of grief and offer strategies for processing your emotions and letting go of the past.

Navigating the Stages of Grief

Grief is not a linear process, and it can manifest differently for each person. However, it often follows a pattern of stages, which were first outlined by psychiatrist Elisabeth Kübler-Ross:

1. Denial: Initially, you may find it hard to believe that the marriage is over. You might deny the reality of the situation, hoping for reconciliation or clinging to what once was.

2. Anger: As reality sets in, anger can arise. You may feel anger toward your ex-spouse, yourself, or the circumstances that led to the divorce. This anger is a natural part of the healing process.

CHAPTER 4: GRIEVING AND LETTING GO

3. Bargaining: In this stage, you might try to make deals or bargains with a higher power or even your ex-spouse in an attempt to reverse the divorce. This is a way of coping with the loss and seeking control.

4. Depression: Feelings of deep sadness and despair can be overwhelming. You may struggle with the weight of the loss and the changes it brings to your life.

5. Acceptance: Ultimately, with time and support, most people reach a point of acceptance. This doesn't mean you have to like or agree with the divorce, but you find a way to acknowledge it and move forward.

Strategies for Processing and Acceptance

1. Allow Yourself to Feel: Grief is a natural response to loss, and all emotions, including the painful ones, are valid. Give yourself permission to feel the sadness, anger, and confusion. Avoid suppressing or numbing your emotions.

2. Seek Support: Lean on your support system, whether it's friends, family, or a therapist. Talking about your feelings and experiences can provide relief and help you process your emotions.

3. Express Yourself: Consider journaling, art, or other creative outlets as a means of expressing your feelings. Sometimes, putting your emotions into words or art can be cathartic.

4. Practice Self-Compassion: Be patient and gentle with yourself. Avoid self-blame and self-criticism. Remember that healing takes time, and it's okay to ask for help.

5. Create New Rituals: Letting go of the past can be facilitated by creating new rituals or traditions that mark your transition into this new phase of life. This can help you focus on the future instead of dwelling on the past.

6. Professional Help: If you find yourself stuck in one stage of grief or unable to cope with intense emotions, consider seeking help from a therapist who specializes in grief and loss.

Remember that grieving and letting go is a highly individual process, and there is no set timeline for how long it should take. Embrace your emotions and trust that, in time, you will find a way to move forward with a sense of acceptance and renewed strength. In the following chapters, we will explore more aspects of emotional healing after divorce to support your journey towards a brighter future.

5

Chapter 5: Rediscovering Your Identity

Divorce often leaves individuals feeling like they've lost a part of themselves along with the marriage. Reclaiming your sense of self and identity is a vital step in the process of emotional healing after divorce. In this chapter, we'll explore the journey of self-discovery and provide guidance on how to reconnect with your individuality and self-worth.

The Loss of Self in Divorce

It's not uncommon to feel like your identity is closely tied to your role as a spouse and partner. When that role changes or dissolves through divorce, it can leave you questioning who you are outside of the marriage. This can be disorienting and even unsettling, but it's also an opportunity for personal growth and rediscovery.

Exploring Your Interests and Passions

1. Reflect on Your Past: Take time to reflect on the interests, hobbies, and passions you may have set aside during your marriage. What activities used to bring you joy and fulfillment? What did you enjoy doing before the relationship?

2. Try New Things: Don't be afraid to experiment with new activities and experiences. This can be an exciting way to discover hidden talents or interests you never knew you had.

3. Set Personal Goals: Establish achievable goals for yourself. These can be related to personal development, career, or hobbies. Having goals to work toward can give you a sense of purpose and accomplishment.

4. Reconnect with Old Friends: Reach out to friends you may have lost touch with during your marriage. Reconnecting with old friends can remind you of who you were before the relationship and offer valuable support.

5. Seek Professional Guidance: If you're struggling with identity issues or a sense of emptiness, a therapist or counselor can provide guidance and support in the process of self-discovery.

Embracing Independence and Self-Worth

Rediscovering your identity also involves cultivating a strong sense of self-worth and independence:

1. Practice Self-Compassion: Be kind and patient with yourself as you embark on this journey. Self-discovery can be both rewarding and challenging, and it's okay to have setbacks.

2. Set Healthy Boundaries: Define your personal boundaries and communicate them clearly. This includes setting boundaries with your ex-spouse, friends, and family to protect your newfound sense of self.

3. Learn from the Past: Reflect on what you've learned from your previous relationship. Consider the strengths and weaknesses of the partnership, and use these insights to inform your future choices.

4. Celebrate Your Achievements: As you explore new interests and passions, celebrate your achievements, no matter how small they may seem. Each step forward is a testament to your resilience and growth.

5. Nurture Self-Confidence: Confidence often grows when you step out of your comfort zone. Embrace challenges and believe in your ability to adapt and thrive.

Rediscovering your identity after divorce is an empowering process. It's an opportunity to build a life that aligns with your values and desires. While the journey may have its ups and downs, it ultimately leads to a deeper understanding of yourself and a stronger sense of self-worth. In the chapters ahead, we'll continue to explore various aspects of emotional healing after divorce to help you reclaim your inner strength and build a brighter future.

6

Chapter 6: Coping with Change and Uncertainty

Divorce brings profound changes and uncertainty into your life. Adapting to this new reality can be challenging, but it's also an opportunity for growth and transformation. In this chapter, we will explore the practical aspects of navigating change and uncertainty post-divorce and offer strategies to help you embrace this transformational phase.

Dealing with Practical Changes

Divorce often triggers a series of practical changes in your life, such as:

- Living Arrangements: You may need to find a new place to live, potentially downsizing or adjusting to a different living situation.

- Financial Adjustments: Your financial situation may change significantly, requiring you to create a new budget and financial plan.

- Co-Parenting Responsibilities: If you have children, co-parenting dynamics will evolve, necessitating clear communication and shared decision-making.

CHAPTER 6: COPING WITH CHANGE AND UNCERTAINTY

- Social Circles: Relationships with mutual friends and family may shift, and you may need to create new social circles and support networks.

Embracing Uncertainty as an Opportunity

1. Focus on the Present: Instead of dwelling on the uncertainties of the future, concentrate on the present moment. What can you do today to improve your life or find contentment?

2. Set Short-Term Goals: Break down long-term objectives into smaller, manageable goals. This can make the path forward feel less daunting and more achievable.

3. Cultivate Flexibility: Be open to change and willing to adapt. Flexibility allows you to navigate unexpected challenges with resilience.

4. Seek Professional Advice: Consult with financial advisors or legal experts to ensure you make informed decisions regarding property, assets, and legal matters.

5. Create a Support System: Lean on your support network for guidance and emotional support during uncertain times. Sometimes, simply talking through your concerns can provide clarity.

Reinventing Yourself

Divorce presents an opportunity for reinvention and personal growth:

1. Explore New Interests: Use this time to explore hobbies, interests, or career paths you may have set aside during your marriage.

2. Invest in Self-Improvement: Consider furthering your education or acquiring new skills to boost your confidence and expand your opportunities.

3. Seek Professional Development: If you're returning to or entering the workforce, invest in professional development to enhance your career prospects.

4. Cultivate Resilience: Building resilience is essential for coping with change and uncertainty. Embrace challenges as opportunities to grow stronger.

5. Practice Gratitude: Cultivate gratitude for the positive aspects of your life. It can help shift your perspective from what's lost to what remains and what can be gained.

Navigating change and uncertainty post-divorce is undoubtedly challenging, but it also offers a chance for personal reinvention and growth. Embrace the unknown as an opportunity to create a life that aligns more closely with your values and aspirations. In the upcoming chapters, we'll continue to explore various aspects of emotional healing after divorce to guide you toward a brighter and more fulfilling future.

7

Chapter 7: Healing through Forgiveness

Divorce often leaves emotional scars, and one of the most powerful tools for healing those wounds is forgiveness. While it may seem difficult or even impossible, forgiveness is a transformative process that can set you free from the burdens of anger, resentment, and pain. In this chapter, we will explore the concept of forgiveness and provide strategies for forgiving both your ex-spouse and, perhaps most importantly, yourself.

The Power of Forgiveness

Forgiveness is not about condoning hurtful actions or invalidating your own feelings. Instead, it's a process of releasing the emotional grip that past events may have on you. Here's why forgiveness is essential:

1. Emotional Liberation: Forgiveness allows you to let go of negative emotions, such as anger, resentment, and bitterness, which can be emotionally exhausting.

2. Personal Growth: It's an opportunity for personal growth and healing. Forgiveness can lead to increased self-esteem, empathy, and resilience.

3. Improved Relationships: If you have children together or need to maintain

some form of contact with your ex-spouse, forgiveness can help facilitate healthier communication and co-parenting.

Forgiving Your Ex-Spouse

1. Acknowledge Your Feelings: Before you can forgive, it's crucial to acknowledge and process your emotions. Understand that forgiveness doesn't mean you have to forget or justify what happened.

2. Empathize: Try to put yourself in your ex-spouse's shoes and understand their perspective. This doesn't excuse their behavior, but it can help you empathize with their humanity.

3. Release Resentment: Holding onto resentment only prolongs your own suffering. Make a conscious choice to release the negative emotions tied to your ex-spouse's actions.

4. Set Boundaries: If necessary, set clear boundaries with your ex-spouse to protect yourself emotionally and establish a respectful co-parenting relationship.

Forgiving Yourself

Forgiving yourself is often the most challenging part of the process, but it's equally important:

1. Self-Reflection: Reflect on your role in the relationship and the divorce. Understand that you are not solely to blame, and it takes two people to make or break a marriage.

2. Practice Self-Compassion: Treat yourself with the same kindness and understanding that you would offer a friend. You're human and allowed to make mistakes.

CHAPTER 7: HEALING THROUGH FORGIVENESS

3. Learn and Grow: Instead of dwelling on past regrets, focus on what you've learned from the experience. Use it as an opportunity for personal growth and self-improvement.

4. Let Go of Guilt: Guilt can be paralyzing. Recognize that you did what you believed was right at the time, and forgiveness allows you to move forward.

The Journey of Forgiveness

Forgiveness is a journey, not a destination. It may not happen overnight, and that's okay. The process is unique to each person and situation. Some individuals may find solace in forgiveness relatively quickly, while others may need more time and introspection.

In the chapters ahead, we will continue to explore various aspects of emotional healing after divorce, including rebuilding trust, setting new goals, and embracing a brighter future. Forgiveness is a profound step on the path to healing, offering you the opportunity to reclaim your inner strength and find peace.

8

Chapter 8: Co-Parenting and Communication

Co-parenting after divorce can be one of the most challenging aspects of the process, yet it's crucial for the well-being of your children and your own emotional healing. Effective communication and cooperation with your ex-spouse are key to making co-parenting work. In this chapter, we will explore strategies for navigating co-parenting dynamics and fostering healthy communication.

The Importance of Co-Parenting

Co-parenting involves working together with your ex-spouse to raise your children, despite the end of your romantic relationship. Here's why co-parenting is essential:

1. Stability for Children: Co-parenting provides stability and consistency in your children's lives, which is crucial for their emotional well-being.

2. Shared Responsibilities: Sharing parenting responsibilities ensures that both parents play an active role in their children's upbringing.

CHAPTER 8: CO-PARENTING AND COMMUNICATION

3. Reducing Conflict: Effective co-parenting can minimize conflict, which benefits both you and your children.

Strategies for Successful Co-Parenting

1. Open and Honest Communication: Establish clear and open channels of communication with your ex-spouse. Keep discussions focused on the well-being of your children.

2. Create a Co-Parenting Plan: Develop a comprehensive co-parenting plan that outlines custody arrangements, visitation schedules, and important decisions regarding your children's upbringing.

3. Be Flexible: Life is unpredictable, and circumstances may change. Be willing to adjust your co-parenting plan when necessary, while keeping your children's best interests in mind.

4. Respect Boundaries: Respect each other's boundaries and personal lives. Avoid prying into each other's personal affairs and maintain a sense of independence.

5. Stay Child-Centered: Always prioritize the needs and best interests of your children over any personal conflicts or disagreements.

6. Positive Communication: Use positive and constructive language when communicating with your ex-spouse. Avoid blaming, criticizing, or using your children as messengers.

Effective Co-Parenting Communication

1. Use Technology: Utilize communication tools, such as shared calendars or co-parenting apps, to coordinate schedules and share important information.

2. Regular Updates: Keep each other informed about your children's activities, school events, and medical appointments. Transparency is crucial.

3. Meetings or Mediation: Consider meetings or mediation sessions to address larger issues or disagreements in a neutral and controlled environment.

4. Embrace Parallel Parenting: In situations of high conflict, parallel parenting may be necessary. This involves minimal direct contact and communication, focusing solely on the children's needs.

Seeking Professional Help

If you find co-parenting particularly challenging or if conflicts persist, consider seeking the assistance of a family therapist or mediator. They can help you navigate communication difficulties and find common ground.

Remember that successful co-parenting is an ongoing process that requires patience, empathy, and flexibility. Your ability to work together with your ex-spouse for the sake of your children's well-being is a testament to your resilience and commitment to their happiness. In the chapters ahead, we'll explore more aspects of emotional healing after divorce, including rebuilding trust and setting new goals for your future.

9

Chapter 9: Rebuilding Trust and Relationships

After a divorce, trust can be one of the most fragile aspects of your life. Trust in your ex-spouse may have eroded during the marriage, and trust in future relationships may seem daunting. In this chapter, we will explore the process of rebuilding trust, both in yourself and in your interactions with others, as you embark on your journey toward emotional healing and personal growth.

Rebuilding Self-Trust

1. Self-Reflection: Begin by reflecting on your own trust issues and any past experiences that may have contributed to them. Understand that trust in others often starts with trust in yourself.

2. Forgive Yourself: If you made mistakes in your past relationship or feel responsible for the divorce, practice self-compassion and forgiveness. Recognize that you did your best with the knowledge and resources you had at the time.

3. Set Healthy Boundaries: Establish clear personal boundaries and commu-

nicate them assertively. Boundaries are a vital aspect of self-trust, as they protect your well-being.

4. Self-Care: Prioritize self-care to build self-esteem and self-worth. When you care for yourself, you send a message that you are worthy of trust and respect.

Rebuilding Trust in Others

1. Take Your Time: Trust in new relationships, whether they are romantic, platonic, or professional, takes time to develop. Don't rush the process.

2. Communicate Openly: Transparent communication is key to rebuilding trust. Be honest and upfront about your expectations, concerns, and boundaries.

3. Observe Consistency: Trust is often built through consistent behavior over time. Pay attention to how others consistently demonstrate trustworthiness.

4. Seek Trusted Advice: If you're unsure about trusting someone, seek advice from friends, family, or a therapist who can offer an objective perspective.

5. Understand Trust Is Earned: Trust should be earned, not given blindly. Allow individuals to demonstrate their trustworthiness through their actions.

Rebuilding Trust in Co-Parenting

1. Keep Your Promises: In co-parenting, consistency and reliability are crucial. Keep your promises regarding visitation, schedules, and responsibilities.

2. Respect Shared Decision-Making: If co-parenting decisions require collaboration, approach them with an open mind and a willingness to compromise when necessary.

3. Prioritize Your Children: Always make decisions based on the best interests of your children, not personal grievances or conflicts with your ex-spouse.

Seeking Professional Guidance

If you find that rebuilding trust, whether in yourself or in others, is particularly challenging or if past traumas are interfering with your ability to trust, consider seeking the help of a therapist or counselor. They can provide guidance and support tailored to your specific trust-related issues.

Remember that rebuilding trust is a gradual process that may involve setbacks. Be patient with yourself and others, and approach trust-building with an open heart and a willingness to learn and grow. In the chapters ahead, we will continue to explore various aspects of emotional healing after divorce, including setting new goals and embracing a brighter future. Trust is a foundation for healthy relationships, and as you rebuild it, you pave the way for a more fulfilling life.

10

Chapter 10: Financial Recovery and Independence

Divorce often brings significant financial changes and challenges. Rebuilding your financial stability and independence is a crucial aspect of your journey toward emotional healing and a brighter future. In this chapter, we will explore strategies for managing your finances post-divorce and creating a secure financial future.

Assessing Your Financial Situation

1. Gather Financial Information: Begin by gathering all relevant financial documents, including bank statements, tax returns, retirement account statements, and records of debts and assets.

2. Create a Budget: Develop a comprehensive budget that outlines your income, expenses, and financial goals. This will help you gain clarity on your financial situation.

3. Track Your Expenses: Monitor your spending habits to identify areas where you can cut costs or allocate funds more effectively.

CHAPTER 10: FINANCIAL RECOVERY AND INDEPENDENCE

Establishing Financial Goals

1. Short-Term Goals: Set achievable short-term financial goals, such as creating an emergency fund, paying off debt, or covering immediate expenses.

2. Long-Term Goals: Plan for long-term financial security by setting goals like retirement savings, homeownership, or funding your children's education.

3. Consult a Financial Advisor: If you're uncertain about financial planning or investment strategies, consider consulting a financial advisor to create a personalized financial plan.

Managing Debt

1. Prioritize High-Interest Debt: If you have significant debt, focus on paying off high-interest loans and credit cards first to minimize interest expenses.

2. Debt Consolidation: Explore debt consolidation options to streamline your debt and potentially secure a lower interest rate.

Building an Emergency Fund

1. Emergency Fund: Establish an emergency fund with three to six months' worth of living expenses. This fund acts as a financial safety net in case of unexpected expenses or job loss.

Saving for Retirement

1. Retirement Savings: Continue or begin contributing to retirement accounts, such as a 401(k) or an IRA, to secure your financial future.

Financial Independence

1. Financial Independence: Work toward financial independence by building your career, acquiring new skills, or exploring entrepreneurial opportunities.

2. Protect Your Financial Future: Consider obtaining insurance policies, such as health insurance, life insurance, or disability insurance, to safeguard against unexpected financial setbacks.

Seek Professional Guidance

If you're overwhelmed by financial concerns or need assistance in managing your finances after divorce, consider consulting a financial advisor or counselor. They can provide expert advice tailored to your unique situation.

Remember that financial recovery and independence are achievable goals, even in the wake of divorce. By taking proactive steps and making informed financial decisions, you can regain control of your financial well-being and work toward a more secure and prosperous future. In the chapters ahead, we will continue to explore various aspects of emotional healing after divorce, including setting new goals and embracing a brighter tomorrow.

11

Chapter 11: Setting New Goals and Aspirations

Divorce is not the end of your story; it's the beginning of a new chapter in your life. Setting new goals and aspirations is a vital part of your journey toward emotional healing and personal growth. In this chapter, we will explore the process of defining and pursuing meaningful goals that align with your desires and values.

Embracing a Fresh Start

1. Self-Reflection: Take time to reflect on your passions, interests, and the things that bring you joy. What have you always wanted to do or achieve?

2. Reevaluate Your Priorities: Divorce offers an opportunity to reassess your life priorities and goals. What matters most to you now?

3. Visualize Your Future: Envision the life you want to create post-divorce. What does it look like? What do you want to accomplish?

Defining Your Goals

1. SMART Goals: Create SMART goals - Specific, Measurable, Achievable, Relevant, and Time-bound. This framework helps you set clear and actionable objectives.

2. Short-Term and Long-Term: Distinguish between short-term and long-term goals. Short-term goals are achievable in the near future, while long-term goals may take years to accomplish.

3. Personal and Professional: Consider setting goals in both personal and professional aspects of your life. This balance can lead to a more fulfilling life.

Pursuing Personal Growth

1. Continuous Learning: Invest in personal growth by acquiring new skills, furthering your education, or seeking personal development opportunities.

2. Overcoming Challenges: Understand that setbacks and challenges are a natural part of pursuing goals. Use them as opportunities to learn and grow.

3. Seek Support: Share your goals with friends, family, or a mentor who can provide guidance, encouragement, and accountability.

Cultivating Resilience

1. Resilience: Building resilience is essential for achieving your goals. It allows you to bounce back from setbacks and stay focused on your aspirations.

2. Mindset Shift: Adopt a growth mindset, believing that your abilities and intelligence can be developed through effort and perseverance.

Celebrating Achievements

1. Milestones: Celebrate your accomplishments, whether big or small. Recognize and reward yourself for the progress you make toward your goals.

Reclaiming Your Inner Strength

Setting and pursuing new goals is a powerful way to reclaim your inner strength and create a fulfilling life after divorce. Embrace the opportunity to define your own path and pursue your aspirations with determination and resilience.

In the chapters ahead, we will continue to explore various aspects of emotional healing after divorce and provide guidance on embracing a brighter and more fulfilling future. Remember that your journey is unique, and your goals are your own. With vision, determination, and self-belief, you can create a life that aligns with your deepest desires and values.

12

Chapter 12: Embracing a Brighter Tomorrow

As you reach the final chapter of this guide, remember that your journey through divorce is a testament to your resilience and strength. While it may have been a challenging and emotional experience, it has also provided an opportunity for personal growth and transformation. In this chapter, we will explore the mindset and strategies to help you embrace a brighter future full of hope, purpose, and joy.

The Power of Mindset

1. Positive Outlook: Cultivate a positive outlook on life. Believe that your future holds promise and opportunities for happiness.

2. Gratitude: Practice gratitude daily by acknowledging the positive aspects of your life, no matter how small they may seem.

Finding Purpose and Passion

1. Rediscover Your Passions: Reconnect with hobbies and interests that bring you joy and fulfillment. Pursue them with enthusiasm.

2. Volunteer and Give Back: Consider giving your time and talents to a cause you care about. Helping others can provide a sense of purpose and satisfaction.

3. Set New Goals: Continuously set and work toward new goals that inspire and challenge you. Your aspirations give you a sense of direction and purpose.

Nurturing Relationships

1. Strengthen Existing Bonds: Invest in your relationships with friends and family. These connections can provide invaluable support and companionship.

2. Open to New Relationships: Be open to forming new friendships and, if you're ready, consider the possibility of a new romantic relationship.

Self-Care as a Lifestyle

1. Self-Care Routine: Make self-care an ongoing part of your life, not just a response to difficult times. Prioritize self-care to maintain emotional well-being.

2. Balance: Strive for a balanced life that includes physical health, emotional well-being, social connections, and personal growth.

Seeking Professional Help

1. Therapy and Counseling: If you find yourself struggling with lingering emotional issues or mental health concerns, don't hesitate to seek therapy or counseling. Professional support can be instrumental in your ongoing healing journey.

Embracing Change and Uncertainty

1. Adaptability: Cultivate the ability to adapt to change and uncertainty. Life is ever-evolving, and your resilience in the face of uncertainty will serve you well.

Reflecting on Your Journey

1. Acknowledge Your Growth: Take a moment to reflect on how far you've come since the beginning of your divorce journey. Celebrate your personal growth and achievements.

2. Embrace Your Strength: Recognize the inner strength that carried you through the challenges of divorce. You are stronger and more resilient than you may have thought.

Moving Forward with Confidence

As you conclude this guide, remember that your journey of emotional healing after divorce is ongoing. Embrace each day with confidence, knowing that you have the inner strength and resilience to create a bright and fulfilling future. Your story is far from over, and the best chapters are yet to come. You have the power to shape your destiny, find joy, and create a life that aligns with your deepest desires and values.

www.ingramcontent.com/pod-product-compliance
Lightning Source LLC
Chambersburg PA
CBHW072022290426
44109CB00018B/2319